Poitry

A Selection Of Poems

By

Simon Carver

Less is the new black...

WhereWithAll Global Publishing 2014

ISBN: 1507640579
ISBN-13: 978-1507640579

For John Antony Carver
All too short a time and so much missed

Contents

Poem

"I am a Poem,"
Said the blank page
White and crispy clean
Looking up and coolly staring
Me in the eyes

"I am pure, untarnished
Objective and clear of purpose
But I can see you
Poet
Or so you like to call yourself
Drunk at parties
And struggling for a pull"

Pixel Perfect

How can art really be
Art
Without the telling
Imperfection
Of humanity?

Plugged In

Pausing briefly
To remove and replace my headphones
And catch the tail
End of the announcement I
Switch on
My brain defaulting to stand-by
And with it the glowing green bite
Of my 6G iPAQ eReader-iPhone
To tweet and shriek
The mundane claptrap
Of
The 21st Century

Into Character

Dawn breaks over the unmoulded raw clay of just waking and
Conscious
Vulnerable realisation washes up in
A rush of memory
Near panic
Curling up tight under the crushing hot sweat press of fear
Frozen

After an age
The alarm punches an air hole
Wrenching
Forcing
The motions of routine
But loosing foul retching butterflies to linger on the edge
Tightening

Breakfast with the children
And *Today* restore
Enough to leave the house
Where once back into the light
Outside
A cold sun quickly warms every overly rehearsed step up
Into character
On to the office from stage right
And someone else's life
Work

The Dury's Out

I had just switched on the kettle
When I felt a presence
Behind
Over my shoulder
Looking over
Oi oi
Can you 'ear me?
Can you 'ear me?
Can you fuckin' 'ear me?
Familiar
Velvet east end
From Harrow

Awight?
Bad day? Old son

It was his third visit in a fortnight
Things must be bad
They were
Yes, bad day, Ian
But what to do?

Let the fancy take you
Old boy and
Fuck 'em
Playful twinkle, smirk
Arseholes
Barstards
Fuckin' cunts and pricks
Two sugars, by the way
And what about a biscuit?

Work Rest & Play

A Mars a day
Is a slick
Faithful
Bar
Of salty sweet
Nostalgia

Power Games

He wears a black peaked cap
But she prefers the helmet with a spike

He favours the swish of the slipper
But she likes to crack the whip

He is ready for anything
But she has to set the time

He wants to grip the body
But she would rather hold the mind

He puts on leather jackboots
But she conquers with her heels

He looks at other women
But she can only imagine another man

He wants to make her feel
But she is only there to grind

He lets her ride on top
But she is content to power behind

Their games

I Have Heard...

I have heard that
They have started to produce many
Flavoured condoms

And I must say
I was not aware of
Vaginas
Having a sense of taste

Ego Rap

You can be a jail-bird, love-bird, honey-sucking humming bird,
Or a quick cat, Kit Kat, quick kit and snacking cat;
Be a rock-bird, shock-bird, grooving loose and boozing bird;
But a wild-style, high-style, likely lad dressing bad can only be a
Strutting good, looking-good-Looker like me
Motherfucker

They Say...

They say that condoms
Are tested
Electronically

And I must say
I have never heard of
A computer
Getting pregnant

On The Bus

"Reet, back forra shower
An' then into us playboy duds
An' off we go"

"A shou-wer?"

"Well, not a shou-wer, lah'k,
Ah mean ah 'ad a bath last neet
Bur ah wan tuh wahsh me fairce lah'k."

"A sausage sarni
An' into uz playboy duds
An' dahn town"

"Aye, dahn town
An' see wha weh can get"

"See 'oo weh can get
Dahn town"

"Gerras much as weh can"

"Like 'er, dahn theeah
See uh?"

"Aye, nah she's fit"

"Reet fookin' fit
Tha' wun"

"An' smahrt"

"A sophisticairted woman"

"Ah'd give 'er one"

"Bet she knows a thing uh two"

"Lah'k a fookin' trairn, mairt"

"Aye, tha's reet theeah
That's wha' rah want
A reet fookin' sophisticairted woman"

So Thin Sophie

Dropping dead gorgeous
If you like translucent skin
But hanging in the wrong places
Elsewhere
If seen
Pulled tight over cheek
Tearing around her chin
Here comes So Thin Sophie
Every fund manager's dream

Now watch Sophie on the school run
Little darlings well in tow
Out by a dotted eight oh six
Chelsea-ploughing up the road
Herding by the gate with the other trophy mums
Not a blonde brain between them,
But good at doing the sums

It's all so very social Sophie
Awfully rude to refuse
Luncheon supper every day
With me time later in the loo
But now we're off to Harvey Nicks
For a little shopping with the girls
Filling those hours before picking up
With more life non-essentials

But what of the airbrushed world outside
Sophie why not open your eyes
Look past the tip of your broker-belt nose
At some of those other lives
You see there's so more to life than big bonus skinny
And a latte on the move
But isn't it amazing what one consumes
When one doesn't really do food

Bony fucking bitch

From The Bus

"Eh look
Quick or yu'll miss 'im
Oo's that?
'Ee duz lok like sumboddeh dun't 'ee?"

"Ooh yeah, that's that Richard, in't it?
Or iz it tha' Paul?"

"Nor, 'ee's bigger than tha', but
'Eh duz look like sumboddeh dun't 'ee?"

"Ooh, 'ee duz look nice, dun't 'ee?"

"Ooh yeah
Bu' c'mon, 'oo duz 'ee look like?"

"Ah dunno
Bu' yuh right
'Ee duz look like sumboddeh"

Accessible Poem

Open
Wide

And say
Ah

Ode to Success

Yes
It's good alright
But you can't
Make a living at it
Can you?

What Do You Do?

"What do you do?"

Came the deep voice of distant relative enquiry
Weighed heavy by years of acceptance
And at once I understood the dread implication
And demand of Adulthood
So
I answered with a smile

"I play guitar and I write and
Sometimes
When the inclination takes me
I paint"

"Yes, but what do you do?"

Ah
You mean what pays the bills?

"I work in a record shop"

Now a glimmer of understanding
Nearly recognition
A port of safety
In the hazardous gale-swept seas of
Youth

Retail
The high street
Named companies and potential
For business
Promotion and management
Countries abroad
Finally the board and
Who knows?
Tomorrow the world

"No
I just work in a shop"

Again
And with every life raft
Offered
The wrong answer

"Ah"

I Was That Talentless Bass Player

Tuning out of the
Bored Meeting around me
I feel
The rock star deep inside
Kick
Listlessly
Rattling the cage
To test the locks
One by one then
Scream silently
To a deafening de-tuned power chord
Of lost record deals, drug-fuelled orgies and
Wrecked hotel rooms dashed
Hope
Just dying
To climb out
To come out
To get out
And
Live

Mind?

You and I
Are spending

Too much
Time
In my mind for

Our own
Good

Paranoia

"Everything is okay
Isn't it?"

"Yes,
But it's hard to hear you
With your hands
Over my ears"

Hurt Wrench

It is very hard to watch
Screen lovers
At play
And wonder with all my heart
With whom you're going to stay
Tonight
And whether you will offer
The same
Caresses
With which you once
Loved me

Mis-match

You had years
Where I had experience

You were looking for a future
I was looking at the present

You claimed the need of values
While I claimed indifference

You had to analyse
But I was reluctant to probe

You set fast on similarity
I thrived on difference

You were forced to evolve conclusions
Where for me the path was pure

You could never quite feel at ease
But I was always sure

For you it meant a simple decision
For me it meant the end of the world

Ageing Faces Facing Ageing

Age means not visiting
My favourite place quite as often as I
Or, indeed, you would like
But, when inclined to travel
Making rather longer
Well practiced and more substantial trips
Thrust full of quality
Time
And always
Lingering lovingly to
A very fine end

Miss You Terribly

Every time
Elvis, Johnny or Don
Fill the air
With raw churning loss reaching
Life
I feel you
Enter the room
And put your arm around me
Dad

December Morning

Low winter sun
Splinters blinding shards
Fractured light through mist

Not A Haiku

Dark brooding skies
Burst bright with relief
Raindrops scattering heaven

Colours

I was once red
And then I was blue
Passing through green
To become something in between
Stopping a while
But then on to age
And safety in grey
Barely a shade
Away from the
No fill of death

Rain

Rain
Refreshes the parts
Other natural phenomena
Cannot reach

Scream

So it is 2014 and here we are
Drowning
In the future of the Twenty-First Century
All twiddling our thumbs and fiddling on and on in
The crazed dog heat of the promised land
While the goths hammer at the gates and books burn
In a world forever mad with the rage of gods

Life
As we know it
It seems
Full throttle backwards into the rich odyssey of the
New Millennium
Ever sidestepping hope to return to an age of plagues
With the dead and the dispossessed trailing
All the way to Mars
Lost in time and one great, impotent tweet

And there we have it
My dearest brothers and sisters
2001 and 2010 have been and gone
Leaving Moonbase Alpha far behind
And now
Just five short years from Blade Runner
We look fully set
To boldly go nowhere
In a galaxy far, far away
Being so very much
Not
One race
One humanity
Out amongst the stars

Porn Shops

A little hard up
Great Aunt Edna
Resorted to pawning

And got £2.50
For a quick wank
And a feel of her tits

Poitry

"And now we're going to read some
Poitry," said the teacher
And I wondered what
Poitry was
And if it was like
Poetry
Only different?

About The Author

Simon Carver was born in Sheffield, South Yorkshire. He read English Language and Literature at the University of Liverpool and has spent almost three decades working in the British music industry.

Very much a first selection rather than a collection, *Poitry* spans Carver's writing from what he says feels like the dawn of time to the present day, gathered and scattered in anything but chronological order.

He currently lives in West Berkshire, with much of his time spent in London.

You can catch up with Carver in the following places and spaces:

YouTube:

http://www.youtube.com/user/elegantandwasted

Dailymotion:

http://www.dailymotion.com/ElegantAndWasted

And remember, poetry is the original rock 'n' roll...............

Made in the USA
Charleston, SC
13 February 2015